Allan Gage

shots

50 recipes for little drinks with a big kick!

whitecap

Note

While the advice and information in this book
is believed to be accurate, neither the author
nor the publisher will be responsible for any
injury, losses, damages, actions, proceedings,
claims, demands, expenses, and costs
(including legal costs or expenses) incurred
or in any way arising out of following the
recipes in this book.

First published in Great Britain in 2005
by Hamlyn, a division of Octopus Publishing
Group Ltd, 2–4 Heron Quays, London E14 4JP

Published in the U.S. and Canada by
Whitecap Books Ltd

For more information, contact
Whitecap Books, 351 Lynn Avenue, North
Vancouver, British Columbia, Canada V7J 2C4
www.whitecap.ca

ISBN 1-55285-684-4
EAN 9781552856840

A CIP catalogue record for this book is
available from the British Library

Printed and bound in China

10 9 8 7 6 5 4 3 2 1

Contents

Note on recipes
1 measure = 1 fl. oz.
All recipes serve 1,
unless otherwise stated.

Introduction

There's nothing like a round of shots to liven up the mood at a party. The mere mention of a tequila slammer is often enough to give people a second wind. Shots are actually a very social drink: glasses are lined up along the bar, then drinkers and spectators gather around before the brave few get a countdown and down their shots together. In fact, if alcohol can act as a bonding mechanism, then shots are surely top of the league.

Ring the Changes It is still the lethal tequila that is most often associated with this short, sharp burst of alcohol, and the sight of people proffering clenched fists in anticipation of a dousing of salt is a common sight in bars, pubs, and clubs around the world. However, this ritual of licking salt, slamming the tequila, sucking a lemon wedge then visibly shuddering is not the only shot-drinking activity that is taking place. The range of drinks has increased substantially and become more imaginative, while the connotations of drinking shots are less negative. People have come around to the idea that, just

because a drink is served in a shot glass, this doesn't mean that it has to be drunk solely as a means of becoming inebriated, or that the contents of the glass must taste foul.

The shot phenomenon now includes a sophisticated range of drinks, embracing every combination of spirits and flavors, so that the shot is now a real player on the cocktail list of even the most upmarket watering holes. Barmen the world over constantly come up with innovative new drinks, and the shot is no exception to this. In fact, since it presents a number of limitations due to size and, therefore, potential number of ingredients, it offers more of a challenge and perhaps receives more kudos when a successful new drink is invented.

Shoot from the Hip There is a right and a wrong way to drink shots. Different types of drinks have developed various rituals over the years, uniting drinkers and creating traditions, such as toasting with champagne on happy occasions. And whether it's champagne or vodka, etiquette is etiquette. If one person has bought the shots, then there is often a reason for this and it's polite practice to wait until your host for this round has made any intentions clear or suggested a toast, or simply given the go-ahead to start drinking. If it's a slammer, then slam! This is part of the ritual and it is bad manners to accept a drink then turn up your nose and take pained sips of it. Certain spirits are meant to be drunk in shot measures, and the hit of the alcohol is felt once it has been consumed. If you're not keen on the taste, then sipping will simply make the experience infinitely worse.

A Mix Made in Heaven Certain spirits work well with other spirits, and these in turn work well with other, non alcoholic, mixers. The key to a successful shot is to produce an explosion of flavors that hits the palate in one short burst. What's even better is when two or three drinks that wouldn't be positioned anywhere near each other in any half-decent bar are served together—and taste fantastic! For example, would anyone ever really think of serving vodka and cream in the same glass? Make that a shot glass, make it Baileys Irish Cream, and add a dash

of Amaretto and you've got the truly indulgent B4-12 (see page 44). Does the thought of tequila with crème de cacao make you feel uneasy? Well, when these two spirits are layered with raspberry purée, it's called a Dash Love (see page 64) and it's guaranteed that you won't be able to stop at just one. Layered shots are by far the most impressive type of shots, and you'll often find that a strong, dry spirit such as vodka will be counteracted by a sweet and syrupy drink to offer something unlikely but surprisingly appealing to the taste buds. The idea is to layer the ingredients so

that the heaviest one goes in first and the lightest last. The more slowly you add an ingredient, the less likely it is to break the surface of the one below—and it should (hopefully) sit quite happily on top. This may take a little practice, but it's not really difficult and the results are very impressive.

Take it Easy If you drink a number of shots in a relatively short space of time, then make sure you're with close friends. Shots don't creep up on you slowly like beer or wine, creating a warm, fuzzy glow—they spring out from behind and hit you over the head like a baseball bat and, by then, it's too late. To avoid potentially embarrassing situations and a day with the hangover from hell, pace yourself by having a break in between shots. In this way you can gauge the effects and hopefully remember your evening. Despite the ease of drinking and the pleasant taste that many contemporary shot drinks have, don't be fooled—they are very potent, often combining two or more spirits. Of course, if you're also drinking spirits in between your shots, then you need to be extra careful as your alcohol levels will already be higher than if you

were sticking to beer. If possible, try to choose shot drinks that contain the same spirit as the one you're already drinking. So, for example, if you're on vodka and tonic, then choose a vodka-based shot. By drinking a number of different spirits, you increase the toxins going into your bloodstream and you'll confuse your body. The end result is that it will try to get rid of the toxins in the easiest way possible—and we all know what that entails! One way to make sure that you don't get into too much trouble is to organize a shot party at home, with everyone bringing

their favorite tipple. Then, armed with this book, you can take the helm and try out your skills as a mixologist.

Bartender Essentials Unlike other cocktails, shots don't require much equipment. However, in order to work your way through this book, you will need a few essentials. The first is a set of decent shot glasses. Despite their diminutive proportions, these come in all shapes and sizes, and, whereas tequila slammers are best drunk from a glass that is narrow at the base and widens at the neck, some layered shots work to much greater effect in tall, thin straight glasses. It depends which drinks you think you'll be trying most often, but it's probably worth splashing out on a couple of different types of glasses. Many layered shots need a spoon so that the layers are poured evenly; a bar spoon is best for this as it doubles as a stirrer for other drinks. Every decent bar should have a cocktail shaker (indeed, some of the drinks here demand one), so it's a good investment. And now you should be ready to take the bartending world by storm, impressing your guests with your knowledge and expertise. Enjoy!

Straight shots

Not for the faint-hearted, the following shots can be poured straight from the bottle:

Jagermeister A bitter tasting German liqueur made from a mix of 50 herbs, spices, and fruit.

Goldschlager A sweet, spicy liqueur with real gold leaf flakes.

Vodka Freeze your bottle and your glass for an icy shot.

Tequila Traditionally taken with salt and lemon or lime, and always a great start to a party.

Schnapps A thick, white brandy distilled from fermented fruit.

Drambuie A mixture of Scotch whisky, heather honey, and secret ingredients. Serve chilled in a balloon glass.

Fernat Branca A bitter Italian liqueur containing medicinal qualities of St. John's Wort.

Sake Perfected at 225°F, a Japanese rice wine that can be served hot, warm, or cold.

Absinthe First commercialized in 1805 this aromatic, green liqueur is made from herbs.

Shaken
Shots

Kamikaze

Short and sharp this is a great kick-start to any occasion. A good-quality vodka is essential.

1 measure vodka
dash Cointreau
dash fresh lemon juice Shake all the ingredients briefly with ice and strain into a shot glass.

Lemon
drop

A triple lemon hit will leave you shuddering but the smooth Limoncello should cut through the sharpness.

¾ measure lemon vodka
¾ measure Limoncello
dash fresh lemon juice
dash lime cordial Shake all the ingredients briefly with ice and strain into a shot glass.

Strawberry field

So fruity it's almost healthy —this little drink is crammed with delicious flavors that will make it a definite hit.

1 lime wedge
dash strawberry syrup
1 strawberry
1 measure Absolut Kurant vodka or any currant-flavored vodka Muddle the lime, syrup and strawberry in the base of a shaker, add the vodka and some ice, and shake briefly. Strain into a shot glass.

Bubble gum

A wickedly exotic drink that combines the green Pisang Ambon liqueur with Malibu for a colorful kick.

½ measure Pisang Ambon liqueur or crème de banana
½ measure Malibu
dash fraise liqueur
dash pineapple juice Shake all the ingredients briefly with ice and strain into a shot glass.

Legal high

You don't need to smoke to get high—the hemp vodka in this shot will ensure you feel the love.

dash Amaretto
1 pink grapefruit wedge
1 measure Vod-Ca (hemp vodka) or any vodka
Muddle the Amaretto and grapefruit in the base of a shaker, add the vodka and some ice, and shake briefly. Strain into a shot glass.

Clem
the Cuban

This smoldering combo of quality rum, fresh mint, and apple schnapps will loosen up limbs for a spot of salsa.

dash apple schnapps
1 mint sprig
2 lime wedges
1 measure Havana Club 3-year-old rum or any white rum Muddle the schnapps, mint, and lime in the base of a shaker, then add the rum and a scoop of ice. Shake very briefly and double strain into a shot glass.

Purple haze

Versatile vodka again, where it's mixed with Cointreau and black raspberry Chambord for a sophisticated shot.

1 measure vodka
dash Cointreau
dash fresh lemon juice
dash Chambord Shake the vodka, Cointreau, and lemon juice together briefly with ice, and strain into a shot glass. Add the dash of Chambord slowly at the end; this will settle towards the bottom of the drink.

Muff
daddy

The delicate flavor of Bison Grass vodka and peach schnapps give this fruity treat a real kick.

1 lime wedge
1 measure Bison Grass vodka
dash pear purée (see page 28)
dash peach schnapps

Squeeze the lime wedge into a shaker then add all the remaining ingredients. Shake briefly and strain into a chilled shot glass.

Rock chick

Blackcurrant and peach flavors are combined with a dash of fresh lime to cut through the sweetness in this delicious shot.

1 measure Absolut Kurant vodka or other currant-flavored vodka
dash peach schnapps
dash fresh lime juice Shake all the ingredients briefly with ice and strain into a shot glass.

Alabama
slammer

This is a drink for serious shot aficionados. There's enough for four people here, so gather round and down them in one.

1 measure Southern Comfort
1 measure vodka
1 measure sloe gin
dash fresh orange juice
4 drops grenadine Shake the first 4 ingredients briefly with ice and strain into 4 chilled shot glasses. Add a drop of grenadine to each. **THIS MAKES ENOUGH FOR 4 SHOTS**

Little
last

Enjoy your gin in one hit with this delicious drink that combines Chambord and lime to give the spirit a lift.

1 lime wedge
½ measure gin
dash Chambord
dash sugar syrup Squeeze the lime wedge into a shaker then add all the remaining ingredients. Shake briefly with ice and strain into a shot glass. **NOTE:** sugar syrup can be made by boiling equal amounts of sugar and water together for 3–4 minutes to form a syrup. Store the extra for future use since many drinks call for it.

Flamingo shot

This cocktail owes its name to the subtle pink color achieved by the addition of just a drop of grenadine.

dash sugar syrup (see page 26)
2 chunks pineapple
1 lime wedge
1 measure white rum
drop of grenadine Muddle the sugar syrup, pineapple, and lime in a shaker, add the white rum and grenadine then shake briefly with ice. Strain into a chilled shot glass.

Rude Jude

White rum blends effortlessly with puréed strawberry and strawberry syrup to make a fruity shot that will transport you to the beach.

1 measure white rum
dash puréed strawberry
dash strawberry syrup
dash fresh lime Shake all the ingredients briefly with ice and strain into a shot glass. **NOTE:** Make fruit purées by blitzing the required fruit in a blender or food processor.

Strawberry eclair

There is a real strawberry explosion taking place here, with liqueurs and fresh fruit fighting for the attention of your taste buds.

1 strawberry
1 lime wedge
½ measure Frangelico hazelnut liqueur
½ measure wild strawberry liqueur Muddle the strawberry and the lime wedge in a shaker, add the liqueurs and some ice, then shake briefly and strain into a shot glass.

Papa G

Amaretto is mixed here with lemon juice and a drop of Angostura bitters to create a wonderfully rich concoction.

1 measure Amaretto
dash lemon juice
dash sugar syrup (see page 26)
drop Angostura bitters Shake all the ingredients briefly with ice and strain into a shot glass.

Vocachino shot

Vodka is mixed with coffee liqueur, espresso, and cream. Serve after dinner so that the party goes on into the night.

2 measures vodka
½ measure coffee liqueur
½ measure espresso
½ measure light cream
dash sugar syrup (see page 26)
½ teaspoon cocoa powder Shake all the ingredients briefly with ice and strain into 4 shot glasses. **THIS MAKES ENOUGH FOR 4 SHOTS**

Poppy

Vodka and pineapple are blended together with just a dash of Chambord to create a textured drink with a distinctive color and fabulous flavor.

¾ measure vodka
dash Chambord
dash pineapple juice Shake all the ingredients briefly with ice and strain into a shot glass.

Spiced berry

Warming spiced rum is given a fruit burst with lime and raspberry in this complex flavored blend.

1 measure Morgan spiced rum
dash fresh lime juice
dash puréed raspberry (see page 28)
dash sugar syrup (see page 26) Shake all the ingredients briefly with ice and strain into a chilled shot glass.

PCP

A veritable fruit basket awaits in this little drink and the vanilla syrup just adds to the explosion of flavors.

1½ measures Xante pear
  liqueur
dash strawberry liqueur
dash pear liqueur
dash lemon juice
dash vanilla syrup Shake all the ingredients briefly with ice and strain into 2 chilled shot glasses.

THIS MAKES ENOUGH FOR 2 SHOTS

Absinthe
minded

The mighty absinthe is diluted with lemon juice and Chambord here, but don't be lulled into security—this is one shot that will knock you for six!

1 measure absinthe
dash fresh lemon juice
dash Chambord Shake all the ingredients briefly with ice and strain into a chilled shot glass.

Layered shots

B52

This is the classic layered shot that tastes just as good as it looks, with a wonderful warm, sweet flavor.

½ **measure Kahlúa**
½ **measure Baileys Irish Cream**
½ **measure Grand Marnier** Layer all the ingredients in the above order in a shot glass.

B4-12

Three decadent flavors, layered to give a delightfully rich mouthful.

½ **measure Amaretto**
½ **measure Baileys Irish Cream**
½ **measure Absolut Vanilla Vodka** Layer all the ingredients in the above order in a shot glass.

Cowboy

This one will have you licking your lips with its seductive combination of butterscotch schnapps and Baileys.

1 measure chilled butterscotch schnapps
½ measure Baileys Irish Cream Pour the schnapps in a chilled shot glass then layer the Baileys over it.

Deaf
knees

Layers of chocolate, mint, and orange deliver a powerful kick and an explosion of flavors as you knock back this shot.

½ **measure crème
  de menthe**
½ **measure chocolate
  schnapps**
½ **measure Grand Marnier**

Using a bar spoon, carefully layer the ingredients in the above order in a shot glass, then down it in one gulp!

American
beauty

This Italian-American coproduction is a sophisticated shot with perfect layers.

½ measure cherry liqueur
½ measure Amaretto
½ measure bourbon

Layer all the ingredients in the above order in a shot glass.

Flat
liner

Guaranteed to put hairs on your chest and a warm glow in your tummy, this cheeky shot is made with tequila, sambuca, and Tabasco sauce.

¾ measure gold tequila
4 drops Tabasco sauce
¾ measure sambuca First pour the tequila into a shot glass, then add the Tabasco very carefully over a spoon so that it rests on the surface. Finally, layer the sambuca on top.

QF

Too rude to print the full name, but don't let that put you off! Creamy Kahlúa and Baileys are layered with a dash of melon liqueur.

dash Midori melon liqueur
½ measure Kahlúa
½ measure Baileys Irish Cream Layer all the ingredients in the above order in a shot glass.

Black **Jack**

An unusual pairing of Jack Daniels and black sambuca works well in this drink and makes the perfect chaser for an ice-cold beer.

¾ **measure Jack Daniels or any other bourbon**
¾ **measure black sambuca** Layer the ingredients in the above order in a shot glass.

Brain
hemorrhage

You'll enjoy making this shot as much as you will drinking it, as the grenadine makes its slow, sickly journey through the layer of Baileys.

1 measure peach schnapps
dash Baileys Irish Cream
3 drops grenadine Layer the Baileys over the schnapps in a chilled shot glass. Very gently drop the grenadine on top of the Baileys—it will gradually ease through this top layer.

Boomerang

Two classic drinks—bourbon and Jagermeister—are brought together here in one glass. They don't like to mix but they taste great together.

½ **measure Jagermeister**
½ **measure bourbon** Layer the bourbon over the Jagermeister in a small shot glass.

Angel's **kiss**

A dreamy combination of crème de cacao, brandy, and whipped cream, this shot is crying out to be included in your yuletide celebrations.

½ measure crème de cacao
½ measure brandy
½ measure lightly whipped heavy cream Layer all the ingredients in the above order in a shot glass.

Fire
ball

A showpiece drink for any aspiring mixologist and one not to be served to the faint-hearted.

½ **measure absinthe**
½ **measure Goldschlager**
½ **measure frozen kümmel (caraway-seed liqueur)**

Layer all the ingredients in the above order in a shot glass.

ABC

Luxurious layers of Amaretto, Baileys, and Chambord make this shot extra special and a bit of a looker too.

½ **measure Amaretto**
½ **measure Baileys**
½ **measure Chambord** Layer all the ingredients in the above order in a shot glass.

Moth & moose

A playful twosome with chilled orange vodka layered over passion fruit liqueur. A sweet, intoxicating treat.

½ **measure Grey Goose L'Orange or any other orange vodka**

½ **measure Passoa liqueur or any other passion fruit liqueur** Layer the ingredients in the above order in a shot glass.

Pillow talk

What could be more enticing than strawberries and chocolate? Try this shot and you'll know the answer.

½ **measure chilled strawberry vodka**
½ **measure Mozart white chocolate liqueur**
dash aerosol cream Layer all the ingredients in the above order in a shot glass.

Money
shot

A wonderful contrast of flavors—fresh mint and delicious herbs—with that all important kick.

1 measure well-chilled Jagermeister
1 measure well-chilled Rumple Minze
(peppermint liqueur) Layer the ingredients in the above order in a shot glass.

Slippery nipple

This is another classic shot that's popular in bars everywhere. It is easy to drink, but has a hidden kick, so be prepared to make more than one round of these.

1 measure sambuca
½ measure Baileys Irish Cream Layer the Baileys over the sambuca in a shot glass.

Dash
love

A jewel of a drink with a few drops of raspberry purée between the layers of chocolate liqueur and tequila.

1 measure light crème de cacao
¾ measure chilled tequila
2–3 drops raspberry purée (see page 28) Pour the crème de cacao into a shot glass, then layer the chilled tequila over a spoon. Carefully add the raspberry purée to the surface of the liquid—it should sink and then float midway.

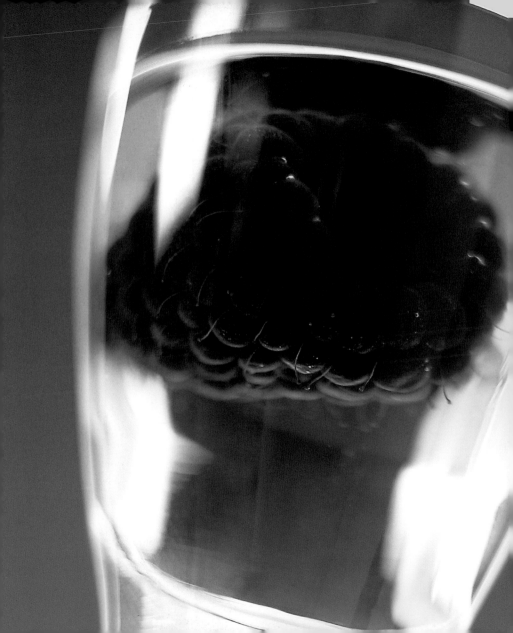

Garnished Shots

Tequila
slammer

The traditional way to drink tequila is to use a tall shot glass with a narrow base and a wider mouth called a caballito (little horse).

pinch of kosher salt
1 measure gold tequila
1 lemon slice Lick the salt, drink the shot, then bite the lemon.

383

A sugar-coated orange wedge makes this drink extra-special. Eat it after downing your shot to round off the experience.

½ measure Frangelico hazelnut liqueur
1 measure chilled raspberry vodka
1 orange wedge coated in raw sugar First pour the Frangelico then the chilled vodka into a frozen shot glass. Serve with a sugar-coated wedge of orange to be eaten after the shot is drunk.

Raspberry beret

A bit of a balancing act but the crowds will love it as the raspberry magically floats between the layers.

½ measure light crème de cacao
1 measure chilled gold tequila
1 plump raspberry First pour the liqueur into a shot glass, then add the tequila. Slowly lower the raspberry into the drink—it will settle between the two spirits.

Bloody simple

Pepper vodka and Tabasco sauce give this shot a fiery aftertaste; a peppery tomato wedge adds fuel to the fire.

**1 measure chilled pepper
(or chili-infused) vodka
Tabasco sauce
ground black pepper and celery salt
1 tomato wedge** Pour the vodka into a shot glass, then add 2–3 drops of Tabasco sauce. Combine the black pepper and celery salt on a small saucer and mix thoroughly. Cut a wedge of tomato and lightly coat it in the mixture, then eat it after drinking the shot.

Passion
spawn

This provides a real assault on the taste buds, with tequila, triple sec, and lime hiding beneath a layer of fresh passion fruit.

1 measure silver tequila
dash triple sec
dash fresh lime juice
1 passion fruit Shake the first 3 ingredients with ice and strain into a chilled shot glass. Cut the passion fruit in half and squeeze over the shot before serving.

Chocolate **berry**

This extravagant blend of vodka, crème de cassis, and dark chocolate liqueur is topped with a miniature berry kabob.

1 measure Mozart dark chocolate liqueur
1 measure crème de cassis
1 measure raspberry-flavored vodka
berry kabob (3 blueberries) Layer all the ingredients in the above order in a chilled shot glass. Pierce the 3 berries on a toothpick and eat after drinking the shot.

Jo-Nut

Vodka, Chambord, and Baileys are shaken together and served in a sugar-coated shot glass with a strawberry to finish.

½ measure vodka
½ measure Chambord
½ measure Baileys Irish Cream
superfine sugar
1 strawberry Shake the first 3 ingredients briefly with ice. Coat the rim of a shot glass with the superfine sugar, strain the cocktail into the glass, and serve with a strawberry on the rim.

Gibson
shot

Not to be drunk if you're trying to impress the opposite sex. Of course you could always ask for two.

dash Noilly Prat dry vermouth
1 measure frozen gin
2 pearl onions Take a frozen shot glass and "wash" the inside with the vermouth. Discard any excess and pour in the ice-cold gin. Garnish with the 2 pearl onions, to be eaten after drinking the shot.

Mint
zing ting

This fresh little number has a green theme with its apple, lime, and mint flavors, and a cucumber finish.

1 lime wedge
2 mint leaves
dash sugar syrup
1 measure apple vodka
1 cucumber strip Muddle the lime, mint, and sugar syrup in the base of a shaker, then add the vodka and some ice. Shake then strain into a chilled shot glass and decorate with the cucumber strip.

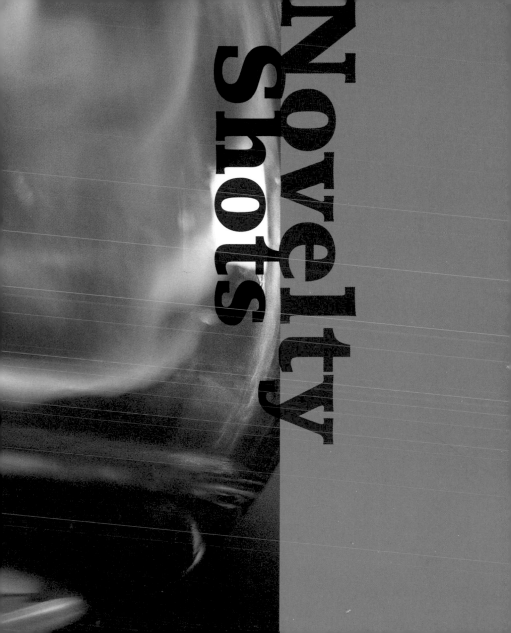

Novelty Shots

Oyster
royale

In this extravagant shot, you "drink" your oyster topped with champagne and let the bubbles go to your head.

1 small, plump oyster
dash crème de cassis
1 measure chilled champagne First place the oyster in the base of a large shot glass then add the cassis and top with champagne. Ideally, drink this while it is still effervescent.

Oyster shot

This is equal parts canapé and shot with a whole oyster, tomato juice, and Tabasco.

1 small, plump oyster
¾ measure chilled pepper vodka
¾ measure chilled tomato juice
3 drops Tabasco sauce
dash Worcestershire sauce
1 lime wedge, squeezed
cracked black pepper
celery salt In a large shot glass, add all the ingredients in the above order, then slowly tip the entire contents down your throat.

Sangrita

Two shots for the price of one: the tequila follows a powerful spicy tomato shot.

1½ measures tequila
1 measure tomato juice
dash Worcestershire sauce
2 drops Tabasco sauce
cracked black pepper
celery salt
1 lime wedge Shake all the ingredients except the tequila briefly with ice. Strain into a large shot glass. Serve the tequila in an identical glass alongside.

Jell-O
& cream

These individual alcohol-infused set shots are the adult equivalent of Jell-O and ice cream.

1 packet raspberry Jell-O gelatin
12 measures chilled vodka
2 measures sugar syrup
4 measures Chambord
cream, to top Cut up the Jell-O and dissolve it in ½ cup boiling water. Add the vodka, sugar syrup, and Chambord to make up 2½ cups. Pour into shot glasses, leaving room for the cream, and chill overnight to set. Top with cream and serve.

THIS MAKES ENOUGH FOR 10 SHOTS

Body
shot

The perfect way to get to know someone a little better —these shots require a partner and you're going to get up close and personal!

½ teaspoon superfine sugar
1 measure vodka
1 lemon wedge Lick part of your partner's neck to moisten it and pour the sugar on to this moistened area, then place the lemon wedge in your partner's mouth. Lick the sugar from their neck, drink the shot, and suck the lemon from between their lips.

Flaming
Lamborghini

This requires considerable skill on the part of both the bartender and the drinker.

1 measure Kahlúa
1 measure sambuca
1 measure blue Curaçao
1 measure Baileys Irish Cream Layer the sambuca over the Kahlúa in a martini glass. Pour the blue Curaçao and the Baileys into 2 separate shot glasses. Light the surface of the sambuca, then instruct the drinker to take a straw and start to drink from the martini glass. As the liquid nears the base of the glass, add both the Curaçao and the Baileys to extinguish the flame, then instruct the drinker to finish the lot. Dangerous but strangely pleasant!

Dram
slam

Only one ingredient, but the way you drink it makes this shot particularly special, plus, it's guaranteed to get you hot under the collar.

1 measure Drambuie Pour the Drambuie measure into a brandy balloon. Swirl it around the glass, and then ignite the liquid inside. Immediately, place your hand over the mouth of the glass, extinguishing the flame and creating a vacuum. Shake the glass briefly, remove your hand, and drink the liquid, then cover the mouth of the glass again. After catching your breath, inhale the Drambuie vapor left in the glass, and relax…

Index

Acknowledgments

Photography © **OCTOPUS PUBLISHING GROUP / STEPHEN CONROY**
Drinks Styling **ALLAN GAGE**

Executive Editor **SARAH FORD**
Editor **JESSICA COWIE**

Executive Art Editor & Designer **GEOFF FENNELL**
Senior Production Controller **MANJIT SIHRA**